THE WAVE OF THE PAST

The Wave of the Past

BY R. H. MARKHAM

THE UNIVERSITY OF NORTH CAROLINA PRESS

Chapel Hill · 1941

Copyright 1941
The University of North Carolina Press

Designed by Stefan Salter

By the American Book–Stratford Press, Inc.

First Printing, March, 1941....... 10,000
Second Printing, April, 1941......108,000
Third Printing, June, 1941........ 5,000

> *"Woe unto them that call evil good, and good evil; that put darkness for light and light for darkness."*

THE WAVE OF THE PAST

1

THE FEROCIOUS ATTACKS and tremendous initial successes of tyranny against human freedom have caused the faith of some Americans to waver and have left others in a state of complete bewilderment. Freedom, some are saying, is a passing dream, whose end has come. Something better, they say, is coming to take the place of freedom: Humanity is moving to a grand new order proclaimed by Adolf Hitler. His cannon are blasting away the old and outworn, his bombers opening new vistas to the future.

How can we know these things are not true? Seeing the failures of freedom and realizing that democracy has often been used as a word to mislead the ignorant or a lure to dazzle the credulous, how can we know where to stand, what to do?

The answer is sharp and clear: We know that freedom has given man the best he has ever had.

We know this by things before the eyes of all who wish to see. We know by a faith that was new, a faith that was the future when the new order, the new tyranny was already ages old.

2

A gifted and nobly inspired poet was in great distress some 3000 years ago, and asked his God for guidance.

He was a Jew and his little nation was being crushed between the two terrible millstones of Babylon and Egypt. His land had been pillaged, many of his people massacred, his state mangled and his God mocked. Evil seemed to be triumphing and right was apparently being trampled under foot. The poet had lost his earth and was on the point of losing his heaven.

So he cried out:

*"The wicked crush Thy people, Lord,
And ravage Thy estate.
Widow and stranger, they murder,
And orphans, they oppress.
They say, 'The Lord will not see.
Jacob's God will not take heed.'"*

In the face of that abysmal catastrophe, he asked in anguish,

*"How long, O Lord, shall the wicked,
How long shall the wicked exult?
And boast of their wicked deeds?"*

He himself gave the answer. It was not very satisfactory but showed that he dared retain his faith in one vital thing.

This was that God was not in league with the oppressor, murderer, and ravisher. Though the poet was a little, helpless man and the member of a little, helpless nation, he refused to give up his spiritual fight; he would not call good evil nor evil good; he would not put darkness for light nor light for darkness.

The thought came to him that perhaps God—his God, Jacob's God, the God of all the universe—was with the invader, destroyer and conqueror, and he drove it away with the cry:

"Can the throne of ruin be an ally of God!
Can he who converts violence into a law,
Who hunts the good man's life,
And condemns innocent blood,
Have fellowship with God?"

The poet refused to debase himself into betraying his vision of Right. He stood alone upon Judea's bleak and hungry hills, beside the broken walls of Zion, and shouted to the enemy empires that they were not of God, that their acts were not good, the future was not theirs.

Then he added, gently but firmly:

"In the multitudes of my doubts,
Thy comfort delights my soul.
When life fell, nearly dumb,
When I said, 'I am slipping,'
Thy mercy, Lord, held fast."

And he said:

> *"Who devised the ear, shall hear!*
> *Who formed the eye, shall see!*
> *Who teaches man, has wisdom!*
> *Who nations guides, brings order!*
> *The Lord leaves not his people,*
> *And casts not off his heritage,*
> *But gives right to the righteous,*
> *To the just in heart their due."*

That faith was one of humanity's supreme creations. An unknown little man, half submerged in the ruins of a world, refused to lose his God and would not call might, right.

About him swept a torrent of exultant power and of triumphant arrogance, that covered all but the peaks of his land. Yet he would not call that terrific flood of sordidness, a wave of the future. He raised high his head and prayed,

> *"Be, God, to me a Peak,*
> *Be, Lord, a Rock of Hope.*
> *Their crimes on themselves shall turn,*
> *To their sins they shall succumb."*

3

More than twenty centuries have passed since then and once more we are in trouble. Or should one say, we are still in trouble. Those have been centuries of much strife, pillage, slavery and deceit. The wicked still exult; they boast of wicked deeds; they crush, ravage, murder and say, "There is no God, and there is no right but the strong right arm!" So we, as the ancient poet, ask, "What does this mean?" We even go so far as to wonder, "Is not what is happening essentially good? Is God not the ally of those who say they are sweeping away the wreckage of the past?"

Some answer their query by saying, "Yes, this is God's deed. This devastating inundation is God's flood, bearing man to a better future. It is God in action; you cannot stop it."

That moral capitulation is the most terrible wreckage of the present catastrophe. It is calling evil good, and putting darkness for light. That is the last and awful blackout. Whatever else we may lose at a time like this, we must not let the last spark of light within us be extinguished. We must not call conquerors good just because they conquer. We must not think a black torrent is flowing upward just because it moves.

As long as we discriminate between light and darkness there is hope. Dark ages come only when the light within us goes out. Tyrants become world masters only when men's hearts bow down, when men call the world of tyrants good and tyrants' tyranny freedom. Men become really slaves only when they sing hymns to slavery. Liberty will not vanish until men begin to laud bondage.

It is the beginning of the end when men write "freedom," "goodness," "purity," "right," "justice," and "God" in quotation marks. That is the same as unfurling in all the breezes of the world the banner of defeat.

4

No one can make a successful voyage unless he understands something of winds, currents and signs in the sky. If he thinks every wind blows toward his harbor or that every current flows toward his port or that every star may be followed, he will surely go astray. If such a one is acting as a pilot, he will lead many others astray.

At the present moment, the world is full of signs and winds and currents. Waves beat thunderously on all our shores. Of course, storms are not new in history. The sea of humanity has always been turbulent. But just now the waves are mightier and the currents swifter than usual. We are facing very acute dangers that have already caused many shipwrecks, so mariners are required who are not unacquainted with human currents.

One of the most persistent and voluminous of

contemporary tides is the yearning of common men and women for a better life. This has grown into a tremendous social urge. In China, India, Russia, Mexico, the Balkans, Italy, Germany, Spain, Great Britain, the United States, almost everywhere on earth, the people are demanding more from life. That is the principal sign of our time. From the last Turkish peasant to the best-paid master worker in a Pittsburgh factory, human beings are arising and trying to move forward. That gives a zest and ardor to this century that many others have lacked.

This social urge expresses itself in many ways: often in nationalism, sometimes in Marxism, again in Agrarianism, in the League of Nations, woman suffrage, in labor unions, in youth organizations, in installment buying, in jitterbug clubs, in hot religions.

This mighty social swell, presaging, one hopes, a springtime for humanity, is due to several causes. One is education. Most children in most countries now go to school; most men and women in a large part of the world can read and write; many, also, hear radio broadcasts and go to movies. They learn how other people live and they, too, want to live better. They are becoming convinced that they were not doomed by God to everlasting frustration.

Strange to say, the world war helped arouse Europe's peasants. They left their villages for the first time in their lives, visited cities, mingled with the city people in the army and other places, saw civilization and began to want beds, stoves, soap, baths, store clothes for themselves.

Democracy also has played a great role, as well as more vital conceptions of Christianity and revolutionary teachings of various kinds. The Reformation, the French Revolution, Socialism, the segregation of workers in large cities, labor unions, mass production, the vast Communist experiment, parliaments, the Spanish struggle, all helped arouse restricted, exploited, underprivileged masses and encouraged them to seek a better life.

This awakening of multitudes in all the continents is one of the most encouraging social phenomena in history. But it would be a mistake to believe that mass strivings of themselves will lead humanity to a good life. There is very little unity in the masses. One cannot even say what the masses are. In most lands they are simply the folks who don't wear white collars and haven't college diplomas. But that means very little. In Russia, the masses used to be called "the black nation"; in the Balkans they are called "the nation"; we Americans call them "the common people." In every case they are made up of diverse elements. Among them are many kinds of laborers and many kinds of farmers, town people and city people, Protestants and Catholics and those of other religions, male and female, white and colored, illiterate and literate. As they all strive for a better life, they constantly come into conflict with one another. Common people unceasingly shove common people around. The masses are not a distinct, solid entity, opposed to the rest of humanity; they are a multitude of mutually antagonistic units, pushing against one another and against outsiders.

A mass surge is very vague. It might be somewhat like an anthill. The ants all move about, but as a mass they stay in one place. The mass wave, indeed, may be like sea waves—which do not sweep forward, but just move up and down. To imagine that the masses are surging forward at this moment, like an escalator or even as a tide rising in a river, is an over-simplification that leads to error.

The mass torrent may end up as a whirlpool, or it may develop into a destructive flood, causing only devastation. Mass surges may consume one another, leaving only wreckage. The struggling masses may be like gamecocks, gouging one another to pieces. They may be an explosion blowing up a factory, a fire devouring a home, a tempest crushing treasure ships.

The Greek cities had a surge for individual liberty, which led to mutual destruction and general subjugation. A religious surge gave terrific power to Islam, that cast a partial blight over three continents. Another religious surge led to the holocausts of the Crusades. A heroic religious surge caused the crimes of the Jesuit movement. A current religious surge in America gives impetus to the Holy Rollers, the Witnesses of Jehovah, and other movements of devout, ardent, misled, spiritual waifs.

A patriotic urge found expression in the K. K. K.; a mighty social wave bore Huey Long on its crest.

How many wise observers believe that the noble

surge of Negroes toward a God that can be experienced finds good expression in making a god of Father Divine? Did America's torrent of longing for a fuller life in 1929 find good expression in the wild stock speculations of those days? A mass surge in itself is no more good than a flood is good or a wind is good. All may be good if wisely used.

Humanity, truly, is moving—it is even on the march, but that doesn't mean it is going any place. Sections of it are marching against other sections. Parts of it are revolting against other parts. A number of selfish and clever individuals have gained control of certain restless bands and are leading them in mad attacks against others.

To believe men are advancing simply because they are moving, is a delusion. To say they are finding the way to the better life just because they are fighting each other for a better life, is very rash. To declare that ruthless chiefs, who have usurped command of murderous columns, are leading those columns to a good new world is evil. To believe what those chiefs say is absurd. Practically every despot in practically every age has declared he was bringing the people blessings. Very few really have. On practically none of the roads which despots have laid out have men and women been able to move upward. It is very harmful to believe that because the Russian, Spanish, Italian and German masses are striving for a better life, the ring leaders of those masses are actually taking them to a better life. That is misreading the signs of the times. It is calling evil good.

5

But how can we tell mass striving that is evil from that which is good?

The past has its mark and the future has its mark. The one is slavery; the other is freedom.

Any wave that brings slavery is a resurgence of the past. Currents of mass longings may give it power, but no slavery-bearing wave really helps the masses advance. It keeps them back. It may be accompanied by beautiful words and glowing phrases; poets may praise it and philosophers extol it; but if it brings slavery it is of the past.

That is why Communism, Fascism, and Naziism are waves of the past. They are broken promises. They are blasted hopes. They are sacred trusts betrayed.

Any wave that increases freedom and self-respect, that enlarges or enriches personality and leads to neighborly co-operation is of the future.

The striving toward free co-operation is one of history's greatest and most persistent currents. It is what gives meaning to history, and value to the chronicles of men; what makes human annals more than the ceaseless repetition of police records. It is this wave of freedom moving through the centuries that makes the times of Abraham Lincoln and William Gladstone different from that of Egypt's Pharaoh Thothmes.

Men have always eaten, men have always made love, and men have always fought for power. Those are old things. Men have put jewels on their fingers and gold chains about their necks; they have placed diadems on their heads or sashes of distinction about their waists. They have always sung in the moonlight; they have joyfully held their boy children in their arms. Rameses' silk was as good as that of Victor Emmanuel and Tutankhamen's gold as bright as Mr. Morgan's. In such things history has done little more than repeat itself.

But there are new things in history. The men who built Rockefeller Center in New York were not the same as those who built the pyramids. The society that founded San Francisco was not the same as the one which founded Nineveh.

Common people have made progress. Let that be shouted from all the house tops. Let proud flags snap that message in all the breezes of the world. Let all the weary and heavy-laden be reminded that through the centuries men and women have moved forward to a better life.

That procession in all the lands among all the peoples has been a movement toward more freedom, more personal worth, more Christian love, toward the emancipation of Demos, toward democracy. That is the wave of the future and there is no other.

That is the new and ever newer. For every clime

and every nation and every race, that kind of change has been the new conception, the new order, the Kingdom of God and of good. Everything else is old.

The new that Moses brought to the Children of Israel was freedom and a measure of self-respect. It was new for mud-spattered laborers to dare raise their heads and unbend their necks. Slave-drivers were already centuries old. Tears of bondage had already flowed in a stream through long millenniums. But liberty was new—even though in a wilderness. For mud-mixers to oppose a despotic labor lord—that was new. For peasants to have their own laws from their own prophet, even though a rough shepherd prophet—that was new.

When the goatherd, Amos, appeared in a royal sanctuary to demand justice and right, protection for the widow, defence for the orphan—that was new, so new it startled all the courtiers.

When Isaiah said there would be a Prince of Peace, who would judge not after the sight of his eyes, nor the hearing of his ears, but with fairness for all little people—that was new.

It was new when Greek farmers and artisans and

merchants, in the strength of freedom, hurled back Persian despots. It was new when Jesus preached that the greatest are those who serve, that men must be as little children, that a human personality is worth more than all the world.

That was glorious, world-transforming news, it was "the good news," the gospel, that has come echoing down the centuries, bringing renewal to each age.

It was new when William Tell and his Swiss comrades defied a tyrant and declared they would be free.

It was new when Italian cities arranged their own governments, when artisans formed free guilds, when John Huss said common men might come directly to the Most High God, when Martin Luther proclaimed that men were the children of God, when the little Netherlands hurled back a world-commanding bigot.

It was new when French social outcasts launched a revolution to create a society in which they, too, would be men, when American colonial farmers became free, when British workers demanded representation in Parliament, propertyless Swedes gained the same franchise as landlords, and labor laws were passed to protect American children.

That has been the new in every land. That has been the dawn, the springtime, the future. That is the one current flowing through the millenniums which is worth recording as history. It furnished the morning song for every epoch: the setting captives free, the feeding of lambs, the helping of little ones over rough places.

Slavery is as old as human kind, but a new thing happened when Lincoln went to illiterate, oppressed, black chattels and said, "Brothers, you too are people; you shall be free." It was new when British reformers went into dark, wet, dirty mines, took dull-faced, bent, ragged children by the hands and said, "Sons and daughters, you are people too; you won't have to work as mules any more; you will not be beaten as animals; you shall be free."

It was new when the emperor of Russia finally went to scores of millions of Russian serfs, dull, sotted, hope-bereft after centuries of exploitation, and said, "You are no longer tied to the land as cows, you are free."

Whenever men and women become people and

feel as people and are treated as people, that is new. When slaves, serfs, coolies, peons are raised to a human status, become our brothers and acquire the dignity of the children of God—that is new!

6

Liberating innovations take very definite forms and find expression in basic new relationships. One of the highest and best of them all is the principle that races may be treated as equals; that there is no "master people"; that a unified nation may be made up of such diverse elements as Latins and Slavs, Celts and Saxons, Turanian and Gaul, of the Nordic type, Alpine type, and Dinaric type, of blue-eyed, brown-eyed and black-eyed individuals.

When the early Christians taught "there is neither Jew nor Gentile, neither Greek nor Barbarian" that brought a new social force into the world. France put this into practice when it assembled people from north and south, east and west and called them all citizens, all free and equal brothers. America invited its children from the Baltic and the Balkans, from green Ireland and the brown hills of Greece, from cold Norway and sunny Italy, from the monotonous steppes of Russia and the vivacious market places of Spain and declared, "You are all members of my family." That was one of the grandest new things the ages had brought forth; it was Christianity; it was democracy; it was what the wave of the future had been preparing 5000 years.

The new also has found expression in a movement toward an equal treatment for all classes. It was new, when workers could no longer be bought and sold, when farmers ceased to be traded in with the fields they worked, when merchants were given an equal standing with soldiers, when landlords ceased to own states as they owned their acres, and princes could no longer take shoemakers' earnings without the consent of the shoemakers. It was new when the apostle proclaimed "there is no bond nor free" and it was as new as the dew of the morning when a society was founded without dukes or princes and in which miners, farmers, milkmaids, school teachers, bankers and landlords all acquired inalienable rights as in a family.

It was extremely new in world history when ordinary men and women, each with an equal vote that could be cast in secrecy and without fear, began to choose their own rulers and direct their own affairs. The right of men and women to make their own laws is also a brand-new acquisition. Until very recent times the masses were exploited by masters, making laws for their own benefits. One of the most firmly established social patrimonies for millenniums was the privilege of the few to impose laws on the many. The law-making monopoly was a ladle by means of which the favored skimmed the cream off the labor of the masses and used it for themselves.

Among the devices used for manipulating the ladles were juridical courts, which were almost always controlled by the mighty. These temples of justice were usually implements of injustice, helping exploiters carry on their exploitation. Then came the new: laws protecting man's person, prohibiting arrests without warrants and preventing princes from apprehending peasants or bootblacks without the approval of judges.

That inaugurated a new epoch in human affairs. Emperors, bishops, ministers and mayors could no longer snatch little men from the street and throw them into dungeons. A man's home became his castle. Judges became the defenders of common people. Individuals obtained inviolable rights before the courts.

On and on goes the story of innovations. Democracy brought something new when it built free schools for all the children of men and let them seek truth and wisdom unhampered by the whims or interests of rulers. It brought a wonderful new gift when it guaranteed each man and woman the right to worship God as each one wished, when it gave disgruntled men and women the right to gather in meetings and make protests, when it assured them the right to write what they believed in books and papers and to promote enlightenment, prosperity, amusement or profit in any club they might wish to form.

It was startlingly new when women and even girls were given the status of human beings, when laborers acquired the right to bargain collectively with their employers and were assured a minimum of sustenance when old or incapacitated or out of work.

Of all the grand new conceptions of human, social, and political relations that democracy has brought, none was higher and nobler than the attempt at a League of Nations, at a Parliament of the peoples that was to have enabled men to beat their swords into plow-shares and cease learning war.

Man's advance through the ages has been slow, and he has had to fight for every gain. Enormous sacrifices have been the price of every forward step. The past has ever attempted to impose a prohibitive toll. And the past has always had to be fought and defeated.

Man has moved into the future with one dramatic victory after another. He himself has been the rescuing prince and he has been the rescued Cinderella. He has opened the doors of dungeons, he has liberated children from bondage, toilers from slavery, dull masses from exploitation, the multitudes from disfranchisement.

7

If you trace the story of the building trade from the Tower of Babel to the New York skyscrapers, of vehicles from the first donkey cart to Cadillacs, of farmers from Euphrates cucumber growers to Iowa corn raisers, of dwellings from the black tents of the Arabs to modern F. H. A. houses, of schools from the superstitions of medicine men to Harvard University, of families from polygamy to Christian homes in Sweden, of children from exposing of infants to free prenatal care—you see ordinary people everywhere moving up into a freer, better life of more respect for individuals. Every bright page in history tells something of human liberation, of toilers, diggers, butchers, fighters being transformed into men and women, of the humble winning rights and speaking with authority. Every happy folk song in every valley of the earth is sung by people who have won their way to a worthier human estate.

Go to every central square in every capital of the world and you will see monuments to the champions of little individuals.

Study the history of the nations one by one, going down the alphabet, and you will find that the new on every page is the story of how men and women and children have won new ways to get more out of life.

You may begin with A for Austria and you will be reminded how a conglomeration of many peoples, how serfs and miners, woodmen and foundrymen, won freedom, created a Parliament, established social insurance, built splendid communal dwellings, erected recreation centers in the woods, put flowers in their parks, sent music echoing through their public gardens, and made of their Vienna one of the ideal cities of the world.

Take B for Bulgaria and you will learn how peasants, freed from Turkey sixty years ago, set up a Parliament, opened schools, covered the country with roads, raised villages out of mud and darkness, created literature, art, music, radically improved agriculture, organized and protected laborers, built pretty cities filled with co-operative homes and made yesterday's wearers of a Sultanic yoke feel as equal citizens in a forward-moving world.

Take C for Czechoslovakia, and see one of the most praiseworthy social creations of the human race. A new, only moderately endowed country, inhabited by three racial groups rather suspicious of one another, made more progress toward general prosperity and individual liberty in two decades of self-government than its inhabitants had made in any preceding century of bondage.

Take D for Denmark and follow a little nation as it moves in seventy years from poverty, exploitation, despondency, and social disorganization, to a way of life that embodies most of the ideals the ancient prophets described in their visions.

Take E for Estonia, little Estonia, that never had but twenty years of democratic freedom in all its history and you will see that those twenty brief springtimes are practically the only bright stars in Estonia's gloomy firmament.

Take F for Finland and rejoice in the story of

a little people, living in a meager land amid unfruitful swamps, that in two short decades of freedom created for humanity a model of the good society.

Take G for Greece, which with all its shortcomings has been transformed by a few decades of even defective democracy.

And so on down the list, through great and small, through backward and advanced. The story of each land will tell of democratic gains, of bondage removed, of fear diminished, security increased, neighborliness augmented, self-respect fortified.

Slowly humanity moved toward higher status. China awoke and so did Turkey, Spain had a Parliament, Germany became a republic, Sweden introduced universal adult suffrage, in Holland every man felt as master of his state, in Roumania peasants raised their heads and workers emerged from mines to help manage their affairs, in Poland long-subjugated masses began to find their way to freedom. Very long and very hard is the way to the good society and to harmony among the nations, but never in all man's annals had he come so near that goal as in the early 1920's. The toil and sacrifices of centuries were then bearing good fruit.

But men are prone to be impatient. Dull of perception and short of memory, we often lose perspective and disdain the very treasures we fought hardest to gain. Men get tired of the good as the Greeks did of Aristides the Just. They lose attachment to freedom, call democracy phoney and Christianity false. They sometimes ostracize the just and hanker after something new, even though it be a despot and old as time.

At such moments we should do well to recall that it is freedom, democracy, and brotherhood which are the eternally new in history. They are the only current that flows constantly toward new shores and never ceases to approach the ever beckoning future. It is they that, in one form or another, have brought man all the good he has enjoyed. And they reached their greatest height some fifteen years ago.

Then man came nearest keeping his rendezvous with right. Then the wave of the future reached its high-water mark, and the sign it left upon the shores of all the nations was: free men voluntarily helping one another. That is the future's seal. By that you may know it.

8

This does not mean that democracy has ever attained its goal. That is unthinkable. There are always new heights to be reached and a great many of them. The future always has a future. We still have prisons to open, bonds to loose, weak to defend, little ones to carry gently over rough places.

The smaller democratic states of Sweden, Norway, Denmark, Switzerland, Holland, Finland had come very near solving some of man's most acute social, economic, and political problems. But the larger democracies, Great Britain, France, and the United States, have not done so well. Deep economic chasms exist between the rich and poor, there is much unemployment, many citizens are dispossessed, a few citizens have too much power.

These defects are vital. They are not only a blot on democracy, but seriously undermine the democratic state. Unless remedied they will destroy democracy. Their permanent existence would be an irrefutable proof of the inadequacy of democracy. The smaller states had wiped them out and shown, to the confusion of the tyrannies, that democracy can provide what tyrants only promise.

It would be provocative idly to praise equality if, in a richly endowed land, multitudes of people were permanently undernourished and poorly clad. It would be mockery to laud self-government if self-government were constantly used by the powerful as an instrument by which to exploit the weak, or to extol elections, if elections habitually resulted in putting gangsters into power. All that is quite clear.

No one may deny that in the United States and Great Britain democracy faces gigantic tasks. Wealth and power must be more equitably distributed, roads to jobs must be re-opened, rewards for work must be more equitable, new Americans must be given a more vital place in the American family, Negroes must be accorded a much more brotherly treatment, housing conditions must be radically improved.

This is beyond the realm of dispute. It is imperative and urgent. Our future depends upon it. To deny or to ignore that we are in need of fundamental improvements is to mock American ideals. Christianity is brotherliness, and democracy is brotherliness. We Americans have a long way to go before we reach a decent minimum of brotherliness.

To realize, emphasize, and act on that truth is very necessary, but it is no less necessary to point out that democracy is the only form of social organization that gives the hope and possibility of such reforms. Social abuses are not especially characteristic of democratic government; what marks democracy is the possibility it gives of eliminating abuses. That is democracy's record and that is democracy's essence. There is no power strong enough to overthrow entrenched privilege and win reforms for the people, except the will and wisdom and sacrifices of the people. They themselves have got to bring about the reforms. It is democracy that gives the chance for that. The people voluntarily working together for social transformations benefiting the people is democracy. That is the story of Sweden, Switzerland, Denmark, France, Great Britain and the United States. Democracy and only democracy enables the people to make real gains for the people.

Democracy is not a status, but a process. Democracy is not a station, but a road. Democracy is pilgrim's progress. Human slavery long existed in America. Indentured white servants were actually bought and sold in America. In the beginning many American laws were designed to favor rich people. But gradually these defects are being removed. The genius of our democracy and of all democracy enables us to keep on going forward.

That is why all who really love their brothers and sisters must retain faith in democracy. To give up that is simply to capitulate. When that is lost, everything is lost, the last hope is gone, the only basis for a better society is swept away.

Christianity as practiced is defective. But shall we give it up? Shall we sneer at it and scorn it?

Shall we turn back to Zeus and Jupiter? Or to Thor and Marduk? We cannot strengthen Christianity's weakness by bringing in a Nero or Nietzsche or a deified despot. We need more love, more neighborliness, more of Christ. What good we have in the world comes from ideals and faith like those cherished by Christians. To scoff at the highest we have by calling it "Christianity" is spiritual defeatism. It is Christianity that bears the good future— not the god Bel or the god Wotan.

The same must be said of democracy, that is, of self-government, voluntary co-operation, personal liberty, and individual self-respect. Without those elements a good society cannot be built. Without such treasures men and women are absolute paupers. What does it profit an army to conquer the world if every man in it goosesteps his personality out of existence?

Every force working to submerge the personalities of common people and make them mere units in a state machine is their deadly enemy. One may laud the proletarian dictatorship of Communism, the corporations of Fascism, the folk-solidarity of Naziism, but since they crush individual men and women they are only Juggernauts. Any autocratic system that destroys self-government, individual self-respect, personal responsibility, and independence of character leads only to the degradation and enslavement of the masses.

First things come first. A good structure requires a good foundation. The only good foundation for a good society is democracy. The first duty of every American is to defend that foundation. If it is destroyed, further building is impossible; if it is preserved, the building on it, even though defective, can be perfected.

Two worlds are in conflict: the world of the past against the world of the future. Every page in human history cries that democracy is the world of the future.

9

A very great preacher, whose teachings were so cogent and whose figures were so striking that they have been preserved twenty-five centuries, once told of some restless, hard-pressed people, who were trying to get out of the frying pan by jumping into the fire. He compared them to a man who was running away from a lion, and a bear met him; then he sought refuge in a house, and a serpent bit him.

Some of our contemporaries are like that man. They are trying to escape from a bear by seeking refuge among serpents.

Democracy, we may say, is sometimes like a bear. It has defects that seem terrifying to some of us. Unemployment, insecurity, slums, graft, political machines, the arrogance of wealth may make some of us feel as though a bear were chasing us. Let us not ignore nor belittle these wrongs. When a man is out of a job, cannot care for his children, has nowhere to live but in a hovel, and sees no decent prospects in this land of plenty, he has good reason to seek help in reforms. He is very wise to try to escape. But he is not wise to run into a house of snakes.

As we look over the world at present we cannot but note that a large part of humanity is trying to escape from something. But, instead of escaping, it may only be running toward a house of snakes. Some of us are hard pressed in our democracy, but autocracy is a viper bringing sure destruction.

Those who say that autocracy is irresistible and that we cannot stop it are making our hard task very much harder. Nothing in human history is more certain than if we want to advance we must first stop autocracy. If we discard democracy and seek refuge in absolutism we shall be throwing away the most vital gains mankind has made. We shall be going back and down to where we were two centuries ago. We shall be re-building the Bastille. We shall be walking into jail and giving the key to our jailors.

Those who say the "new order" of the dictators is inevitable, that the crimes committed in the name of this order are mere scum on the wave of the future, that it is evil to fight this "new order," may be moved by good intentions. It sounds very reasonable now to ask, did not far more good than evil come out of the French Revolution? Who now can condemn this revolution merely because crimes were committed in its name? Are not Hitler and Mussolini and Stalin leading another revolution which a hundred years from now will be seen as necessary to the making of a new and better world? But let us ask in reply, did men in the time of the French Revolution abandon their consciences, did they lie down and let things go, or did they stand up and speak, fight and die for the things in which they believed?

If the French Revolution brought good to the world, of what did this good consist? Was it not in the destruction of dictatorship, in the liberation of a great people? If it was good then to destroy absolutism, is it unimportant now to prevent it from being restored?

Under autocracy we would not be able to struggle for further advances, but would have to start again with the old elemental struggle of getting rid of despots. We would not be able even to think of social rights but would first have to fight for the basic individual right of being considered a human being.

Many of us in America long for a day of salvation, but *der Tag* which the autocrats are trying to bring is darkness and not light, even very dark, and there is no brightness in it.

10

It is not words that distinguish the past from the future. The glowing words with which Assyrian, Babylonian and Egyptian rulers were wont to praise themselves sound very much like political speeches in modern election campaigns. People seeking truth and trying to bring truth to others should not allow themselves to be fooled by words.

Adolf Hitler makes the world resound with eloquent declarations about a new order, about folk-solidarity, about serving the masses, about a bright future millennium. He presents himself as the herald and creator of a grand new system for helping exploited people. This is a very, very old line.

Quite a while ago there was a very handsome

and energetic young man, named Absalom. "In all Israel there was none to be so much praised for his beauty; from the sole of his foot even to the crown of his head there was no blemish in him." He was Israel's glamour boy, number one.

He also wanted to be the Mister Big. So he devised a clever way to gain a following. He went to the city gate, where the law court sat to hear cases, and there he met the dissatisfied people who had complaints. He had each one tell his troubles, patted him on the back, took down his address, and said, "You've certainly had a raw deal, but there's no one in this rotten government to help you."

"Absalom said moreover, 'Oh that I were made judge in the land, that every man who hath any suit or case might come unto me, and I would do him justice!' And it was so, that, when any man came nigh to do him obeisance, he put forth his hand, and took hold of him and kissed him. And in this manner did Absalom to all Israel that came to the king for judgement; so Absalom stole the hearts of the men of Israel."

It was no small matter for peasants and shepherds and carpenters to be kissed by the most alluring prince in the realm, whose silken, well-perfumed hair "weighed 200 shekels after the king's weight." These poor, long-suffering people were pretty tired of aged King David's inefficiency and favoritism, so some were ready to accept the "new order," which the eloquent young prince promised. They hearkened unto Absalom.

But history records they were sadly deceived. King David may have had his faults; but Absalom had his ten thousand. Absalom kissed the people only to gain his own ends, not in order to help them. Many had nothing to lose, so joined the clever prince's conspiracy. We may say, "every one that was in distress and every one that was in debt and every one that was discontented, gathered unto him and he became a captain"—a sort of Fuehrer or Duce.

The same tactics and the same words are still being used. It is not sweet promises that make the difference between the wave of the past and the wave of the future. It is deeds, basic conceptions and ideals.

Dungeons or concentration camps are of the

past; freedom is of the future. The crushing of individuals is of the past; respect for individuals is of the future. Violence is of the past; order is of the future. The exaltation of one party, of one nation, and of one class is of the past. Making laws by edict, converting policemen into judges, turning the family into a mere instrument for reproduction, putting chains on knowledge, giving dictates to truth, prescribing rules for God, are all of the past. They are attributes of slavery, spawned in ancient darkness, nourished in the dank prisons of antiquity. They ride on a sinister torrent, springing from the caverns of primitive men. Would not one be blind if he should call such a stream of primeval darkness a wave of the future?

The similarity between every aspect of modern autocrats and ancient autocrats is nothing less than startling. The rulers of most of the totalitarian countries are like Pharaohs come to life.

Take, first, the matter of international relations. In this field, contemporary despots are consciously trying to revive the times of ancient despots. Japan's leaders urge the Japanese to go back to the dawn of history, when the first Japanese Emperor sprang from the gods. Mussolini wants to go back to the time of Roman usurpers. Hitler never tires of talking about primeval German forests and tribes and gods.

Day and night these autocrats boast of conquest, of making their nations lords over the earth, of a superior race, of master men. Their ideal is domination. They speak as though they were declaiming the arrogant inscriptions written by Assyrian kings 3000 years ago. They conceive of no international order except that of slaves and masters, with one people holding all others in subjection.

Their social ideals also are those of a slave society. One man and one group are masters. The masses are compressed into a series of layers, like the stepped pyramid. Each category is fixed in its place. Farmers are tied to the land, artisans to their work shops, laborers to their spades. Practically all circulation in society is stopped. Humanity is organized as bees in a hive or as ants in a hill. Individuals are obliterated by an imperious social machine that is made up not of personalities, but of cogs, bearings, spokes, and points.

It resembles the society of a Pharaoh, who sent

hordes of workers to build his pyramids, attached multitudes of fellahin to muddy rice fields, gave good rewards to a little group of clerks, favored a small but mighty caste of priests, and elevated himself to the position of Almighty God. Ancient society was a ruler-owned machine that crushed most of its individual members; modern totalitarian society is very similar. The "new order" of the German Nazis is no newer than the temples of Luxor, Egypt.

In ancient societies the function of the family was to breed—to produce offspring. Even slaves had a kind of family life. Negro slave families, indeed, were often well protected. Responsible writers have asserted that American Negroes often received better physical treatment as slaves than they do as freemen. They were well fed and kept in good health—that they might breed children. As cows breed calves and race horses, colts. Southern Negroes still use the word breed in regard to themselves. Slave owners preserved slave families that they might provide healthy slave children to toil, to be sold, to be enjoyed. That conception reduced family life to the level of the pig sty. The words which Adolf Hitler uses about the family, mating, and children are like those used since the beginning of time by slave owners. Are people seriously going to tell us that the movement to convert women into human incubators is a wave of the future?

The state of modern autocrats is almost a replica of those created by ancient despots. In antiquity, rulers imposed themselves by force. Might was practically the sole means of gaining and maintaining power. It was the one source of authority. Usurpation was the commonest means of accession to a throne. And the usurper became law-giver, administrator, executive, judge, the dispenser of truth, the agent of God—no, he became God himself. The ruler was the state, was the school, was the church. He held the earth in his left hand, heaven in his right hand and mankind under his feet. Man, servile in spirit and obsequious in mien, bowed in the dust seven times seven before him. Man lived in the dust.

And modern autocrats have created states like that. They came to power like the masters of Nineveh, Babylon, and Persepolis, by conspiracy and murder. Stalin's throne is reeking with blood;

Hitler murdered his comrades to maintain power; Mussolini murdered former colleagues to obtain mastery; Franco was forced on Spain by foreign guns; Quisling was given authority by the despoilers of his land; Tuka was taken from a traitor's cell to be made master of Slovakia; Antonescu is held in power by the ravishers of his people. Except in a few small states, the people of Europe are as powerless to choose their rulers as were the slaves of antiquity.

Laws, too, are forced upon them, courts no longer have real authority, freedom of the person has been swept away, prisons yawn, concentration camps reach out a myriad slimy tentacles and no man's life or property is secure. Possessions are confiscated with less formality than Naboth's vineyard was stolen by Ahab. A band of Party men establish themselves in every town and village and pillage their countrymen, as robber-knights. These knights also have organized their retainers to plunder every neighboring land.

The totalitarian state is the old tyrannical state made more destructive.

The schools of modern Fuehrers and Duces are

just training camps; they are barracks for young Janissaries. For many centuries Turkish Sultans provided free instruction and a brilliant future for the promising children of Christian subjects. These ruthless and able despots devised a sort of diabolical intelligence test, by means of which they selected the brightest boys in the communities of oppressed Christians. They took them to Constantinople, put them in boarding schools, and trained them to be future leaders. These boys, along with the Sultans, were masters of the vast Turkish empire. They were prepared for that role. Each one's capacity was tested and each was given a place worthy of his abilities.

How generous the Sultan was to Christian boys! Though the Father of Islam, he took under his care the sons of infidels. Though of royal lineage, he took the children of the lowest peasants and made them guardians of his throne. He took the very sons of rebellious subjects and entrusted to them his person. What propaganda a sultanic Goebbels could have made of that!

These boys were torn away from their communities and turned against their own fathers and mothers. They were converted into champions of Islam, defenders of oppression and bulwarks of organized corruption. They were robbed of personality and made the eyes and teeth of a predaceous state. That was what a certain type of well-conducted school and carefully devised education did to them.

Of that type is authoritarian education. In that manner are trained "German Maidens," Hitler Youth, black-shirted Fascist youth and uniformed Communist young people. They are not developed into enlightened, free personalities, but drilled into fanatical soldiers of autocratic chiefs. They are trained to be watchdogs and are stationed before the portals of absolutism to devour all bearers of freedom.

In the spiritual realm, autocracy in all ages is humiliation and degradation. Based on slavery, it creates a slave and master mentality, corrupting both exploiters and exploited. It distorts truth, rewards falsehood, grants subsidies to abject obsequiousness, offers prizes to bended knee and bowed head.

Autocracy breeds brutishness and instills hatred.

It advocates cruelty, teaches terror, and pours out scorn on the very idea of brotherhood. It rests on favoritism and feeds on partiality.

Its basic philosophy and fundamental tenets lead to narrowness of mind and hardness of heart. It cries: "Hate Jews, hate Socialists, hate Liberals, hate anyone and anything the master may happen to hate. Hate by order and hate by command."

It cries: "Be haughty, be arrogant, be boastful. Never ask pardon. Never admit you could make a mistake. Put mercy far away."

It cries: "Exalt yourself, worship yourself, make a god of your gang and of your nation. Force other people to worship that god."

It cries: "Scorn others. Despise black people, disdain brown people, look down on yellow people. Divide men into types; proclaim yourself to be of the highest type and belittle all the others."

It cries: "Raise high the banner of conquest, of mastery of domination and dominion. Be supermen, a folk of lords!"

All this is taken word by word from the philosophy with which modern autocrats are flooding the world.

It signifies the utter blackout of spiritual light. It is a super-jungle of darkest antiquity.

11

Surely, it will not be difficult for conscientious men and women to tell right from wrong in this situation. Though the world has many grey days and many grey places with poor visibility, the difference here between the lighter and the darker is so clear that all who wish may discern it.

Autocracy is no revolution. It is not humanity pushing its way forward; rather a stampede has broken out and multitudes are being led or driven down a long slope into dismal swamps.

This is not a revolution for the dispossessed, giving them a better share of the world's goods. It is not a revolution for the insecure, assuring them safety. It is not a revolution for those who hate war, bringing them peace. It is not a revolution for the distraught, bringing them tranquility of mind. This despotism causes more war, more insecurity, more worry, and reduces the amount of all good things for men and women. It increases, rather than slackens, the dizzying pace of life. It does not bring man nearer to the uplifting voice of Nature, gives him no surcease from ever-rushing wheels. It frees him not from the raucous domination of material things, delivers him not from the sensuous, nor exalts the spirit over the body, nor opens a way toward simpler, nobler, less trammeled living.

It offers no solution but force for the conflict between individual desires and the need of social unity; it has brought no synthesis of labor and of capital except through stark coercion; it does not reduce the congestion of great cities, nor remove us from the elbowing of crowds.

There is nothing inevitable about this movement. It does not form part of a grand train of upward-sweeping thought. Mussolini has not uttered one word that will take a place in the great works on statecraft or social organization. Hitler has earned no niche among thinkers or poets or saints or heralds of a better world. He has not one basic conception of which free men during all the coming ages will not be thoroughly ashamed. As for Stalin, no one even ascribes constructive thoughts or ideas to him. The imperiousness of all high ideals and noble conceptions makes the overthrow of these autocrats inevitable.

And most of them are as weak in all other realms as they are in creative ideas. Rarely in all its recent history has the Russian state or nation been of so little importance in international affairs as at present. It has consumed its own power. Fascist Italy has shown itself an empty shell. Mussolini has converted it into a helpless vassal state fawning before the ruthless master of Europe. With his arrogant boasting about mastery the Duce has made a slave of Italy.

Hitler, one must acknowledge, has developed much temporary power. He has used three old conceptions to give Nazi Germany much temporary might. They are national glory, the looting of neighbors, and a mask of social progress. The last he has used as a snare; the other two are no more revolutionary than the campaigns of Alaric or

Attila. Hitlerism is no more revolutionary than a pyramid, or one of Tiglath-pileser's military parades, or a colosseum. And it is no more inevitable than the might of 75 million people organized for conquest makes it. That is a terrific force, but not as strong as 500 million virile, freedom-loving men opposing it. History has shown that merely in swords, a lust for plunder, and a passion for glory there is very little inevitableness.

Hitlerism is a temporary resurgence of a black and bloody wave of the past, carrying slavery and degradation on its crest and aiming to destroy all the good mankind has built through the ages. To call that good, would be to mock God, and ourselves.

Let us see the truth and let us do the right!

12

How may we do the right? First, by putting our minds and hearts right. We must raise the right banner. We must take the right side.

In this issue there are only two sides. No neutral course remains. Each person is either against this wave of the past or he is for it; he either opposes the onslaught of Hitlerism or supports it. If he makes no choice, that is a choice; if he takes no side, he is on Hitler's side; if he does not act, that is an act—for Hitler.

Not all issues are like that. At some cross roads, one may turn left, or right, or just keep on going, or even stop and wait. But at some, one can't. When a boat sinks, every passenger either stays on or gets off. If one can't decide—he has decided.

The road to isolationism is absolutely closed. Every refuge has been swept away. America's fate hangs on this issue. Every adult citizen, whatever may be the motives that direct his decision or his indecision, is on the side of Nazi tyranny or on the side fighting it.

Let us take sides consciously, solemnly, nobly, and not by default.

And having decided aright, let us act with all our might. What does that mean? It means to do everything that must be done. Nothing less. In a supreme struggle, for supreme values, supreme efforts must be made. The exigencies of each day or month will show what must be done.

Without victory in this cause, everything else is vain. Every beautiful American dream will mock us as a ghost; every grand American achievement will taunt us as a cathedral turned into a slave market.

What are our schools, our churches, our homes; what are our courts, our town meetings, our legislatures; what are our radios, our papers and our movies—if slave-drivers rule the world? Every river in our land would be as the bitter waters of Babylon. Our very homes would be places of exile. We would be as spiritual chain gangs manacled by a power we would not muster will to resist, moving in a darkness created by our own desire not to see.

To prevent that will be our first step. Whatever it may cost, we shall take it.

www.ingramcontent.com/pod-product-compliance
Lightning Source LLC
Chambersburg PA
CBHW020754230426
43665CB00009B/591